My Views:

President Trump & His Cabinet

Raymond E. Smith

Published by

SanWay International

91 E. Main Street

Inman, SC 29349

Printed in the United States

Dedicated to:

All Americans who look forward to a successful term with Donald Trump and his cabinet members.

Table of Contents

Chapter 1

President Donald Trump

Approximately 35 years ago, Donald Trump became my teacher, mentor and guide. My wife and I were traveling down through the state of Florida and I stopped at a book store. A book written by Donald Trump caught my eye. I purchased the book.

When we got to West Palm Beach, we took a cruise up the river. I asked the guide about Donald Trump. He told me where his resort, Mar-a-lago, was located. Although we knew we could not get in the gated community, we drove by the entrance.

When we got back home I read the book and learned everything I could about the construction king that was making his way to the top. His father, Fred, was a city inspector for the city of New York. He taught Donald how to inspect buildings to determine whether or not it would be a good investment.

Trump and his father worked together for five years. When Trump went out on his own he was particularly interested in the west side of New York.

Trump was also the developer of the largest parcel of land in New York City, the former West Side Rail Yards which is now Trump Place. On this 100 acre property, fronting along the Hudson River from 59th Street to 72nd Street, is the largest development ever approved by the New York City Planning Commission. There are a total of 16 buildings on the site, with Mr. Trump building the first nine buildings and the other portion of land being sold for a substantial amount. Mr. Trump also donated a 25 acre waterfront park on Trump Place and a 700 foot sculptured pier to the city of New York.

Trump ran into many difficulties when he decided to build Trump Towers in New

York. He fought the city building codes. He also ran into a problem with his friend and business partner, Lee Iacocca who was the CEO of Chrysler. Iacocca sued trump because Trump Towers over-shadowed the Chrysler building.

Trump won because he is a winner. When he announced that he was running for the President of the United States I knew in my heart that he would win. Even when the popular vote looked like was going to Hillary, I knew that some way he would win.

I liked what Franklin Graham said, "Trump won by a miracle from God."

When Trump runs into a road block he

finds a way to get to the other side. He will go over it, go around it, or dig a tunnel and go under it, whatever it takes he will make it happen.

A few years ago, my wife and I visited New York. We stayed one night at the Trump Towers over-looking Central Park. One night was all we could afford. If my memory is correct the basic room rate was $375.00 a night.

We wanted to do some sight-seeing the next day. We asked if we could leave the car there for a few hours. They said the car would have to be brought to the street and then take it two stories down and charge a storage fee. That was another $75.00. It was worth the experience.

The room was marble and copper trim.

Everything was first class. When we were leaving it was raining. They asked if I had an umbrella. I told them I left it in the room. He said, "That's not a problem" and he gave me another one.

I kept the umbrella and a cloth bag with a copy of New York Times which was outside the door the morning we left as a souvenir.

On January 20, 2017, Donald Trump became the 45th President of the United States.

He started out on day one, signing executive orders to make America great again. He has continued to repeal laws that were hindering the growth of America. The stock market increased about 1,000 points at this writing March 3, 2017.

He has gone up against the giants in manufacturing of drugs, Boeing, auto mobiles and other industries. He is saving jobs from being sent to Mexico.

He has started laying out plans for building the wall, border control, repealing Obamacare and controlling immigration.

In my opinion, Donald J. Trump will go down in history as the greatest president that anyone can remember.

If there is one negative that bothers me about Trump; he is trying to run the government like a business. It can't be done.

Chapter 2

Vice President Mike Pence

Although, the Vice President is not considered a cabinet member, I feel that it should be included here.

Michael Richard "Mike" Pence age 57 is an American politician and lawyer and the 48th Vice President of the United States. He previously served as the 50th Governor of Indiana from 2013 to 2017.

Before being selected to run as Trump's running mate I knew nothing about Pence. I was impressed with his speaking ability and positive attitude.

I feel that he is already an asset to the American people.

Born and raised in Columbus, Indiana, Pence graduated from Hanover College and earned a law degree from the Indiana University Robert H. McKinney School of Law before entering private practice. After losing two bids for a U.S. congressional seat in 1988 and 1990, he became a conservative radio and television talk show host from 1994 to 1999. Pence was elected to the United States Congress in 2000 and represented Indiana's 2nd congressional district and Indiana's 6th congressional district in the United States

House of Representatives from 2001 to 2013. He served as the chairman of the House Republican Conference from 2009 to 2011. Pence positioned himself as a principled ideologue and supporter of the Tea Party movement, noting he was "a Christian, a conservative, and a Republican, in that order."

Chapter 3

Secretary of state

Rex Tillerson

Tillerson, age 64, a former CEO of ExxonMobil, is the first secretary of state without government or military experience. He has a decades-long business relationship with Russian President Vladimir Putin, which has raised eyebrows among Democratic and some Republican lawmakers. The vote to confirm Tiller son was the tightest vote for a secretary of state in at least 60 years.

Former ExxonMobil CEO Rex Tiller son was confirmed Secretary of state

Former ExxonMobil CEO Rex Tiller son was confirmed as the new secretary of state by a vote of 56 to 43 in the Senate. Four Democratic and all Republican senators voted in favor of President Donald Trump's pick to be the nation's top diplomat.

Trump settled on Tillerson to lead the State Department after a long and high-profile search.

"Rex knows how to manage a global

enterprise, which is crucial to running a suc-cessful State Department, and his relation-ships with leaders all over the world are sec-ond to none. I can think of no one more pre-pared and no one more dedicated to serve as secretary of state at this critical time in our history," Trump said in a Dec. 13 statement.

Tillerson has ample experience in in-ternational negotiations. However, he also has a history of close ties to Russia and its President Vladimir Putin, which came up during his confirmation hearings.

What he used to do: Tillerson joined ExxonMobil in 1975 as a production engi-neer. He rose through the ranks, becoming general manager in 1989 and production adviser to the Exxon Corp. in 1992. In 1998 he became vice president of Exxon Ventures and president of Exxon Neftegas Limited, where he was responsible for the company's holdings in Russia, including the Caspian Sea and the Sakhalin Island area. In August 2001 he was promoted to senior vice president of the ExxonMobil Corp. and became CEO in 2006. He has no previous public sector experience.

Relationship with Trump: Tillerson emerged as a late contender on what seemed to be an ever expanding list of possible nominees for secretary of state. He met with Trump on Dec. 6, and the two convened for a second time on Dec. 10. Tillerson has a history of donating to Republicans in recent years. According to Federal Election Commission filings, he donated $50,000 to Mitt Romney's presidential victory fund in 2012 and gave $5,000 to Right to Rise, a super PAC backing Jeb Bush, in August 2015. But his FEC records do not show any donations to Trump during the 2016 campaign.

Trump and Exxon relationship: Trump owned ExxonMobil stock. His 2015 financial disclosure filing lists $50,000 to $100,000 worth of assets in ExxonMobil.

Tillerson's business relationship with Russia dates to the 1990s, when he assumed responsibility for all of ExxonMobil's holdings there. In 2011 the company forged a deal with Russian oil company Rosneft, which at that time was 75 percent owned by the Russian government. The deal gave ExxonMobil access to Arctic oil deposits, and Putin attended the signing ceremony. In 2013 the two companies expanded their partnership. That year, Tillerson received the Order of Friendship from Putin.

In 2014, after Russia annexed Crimea, Exxon was forced to halt the deal because of U.S. sanctions. Although ExxonMobil put out a press release saying it was "winding down" its operations after the sanctions, Tillerson reportedly called sanctions ineffective at a 2014 shareholders meeting.

Tillerson's relationship with Russia

was a focal point in his confirmation hearings with the Senate Foreign Relations Committee last month.

He referred to economic sanctions against Russia as a "powerful tool" and rejected the claims that he and ExxonMobil, under his leadership, lobbied against them to advance the company's financial interests.

Although, Tillerson has acknowledged climate change is a problem, ExxonMobil was the subject of controversy at its shareholders meeting last year for rejecting resolutions that would have pushed the company's resources toward renewable energy, according to a Washington Post article.

At least five attorneys general were investigating the company's climate change policies as of spring 2016, including New York's Eric Schneiderman, who oversaw a now settled lawsuit against Trump University, according to the Post.

Trump settled on Tillerson to lead the State Department after a long and high-profile search.

Tillerson's record while serving as CEO of ExxonMobil is a good indicator of what he can do as Secretary of State.

Chapter 4

Jeff Sessions

U.S. Attorney General

Jeff Sessions, Age 70 was sworn in at the White House as the next U.S. attorney general.

The upper chamber approved President Donald Trump's nominee by a largely party-line vote of 52-47. One Democrat, Sen.

Joe Manchin of West Virginia, joined Republicans in confirming Sessions.

Sessions' nomination as the head of the Department of Justice drew significant criticism from Democrats and civil rights groups. In 1986 he failed to be confirmed for a federal judgeship after testimony that he made racially tinged remarks. His confirmation hearings last month were also not without controversy.

Session's Hometown: Selma, Alabama, which had a notable role in the civil rights movement. Earlier this year, Sessions reflected on the historic nature of his birthplace. "Certainly I feel like I should have stepped forward more," he said, reflecting on the civil rights struggle.

Session's Family: He has three children and six grandchildren. He was born to Abbie and Jefferson Beauregard Sessions. His father owned a general store in Hybart, Alabama, and a farm equipment dealership.

Sessions was a senator from Alabama was first elected in 1996 and served as a member of the Senate Judiciary Committee. From 1975 to 1977 he was an assistant U.S. attorney for the Southern District of Alabama and from 1981 to 1993 was the U.S. attorney for the district. In 1994 he was elected Alabama's 44th attorney general.

He supported President George W.

Bush's 2001 and 2003 tax cut packages, the war in Iraq and a proposed constitutional amendment to ban same-sex marriage. He has opposed most major Democratic legislation, including the stimulus bill, the Affordable Care Act and the repeal of "don't ask, don't tell."

He was ranked by The National Journal in 2007 as the fifth-most-conservative U.S. senator.

He worked as a lawyer in Russellville and Mobile, where he still lives. He was a captain for the Army Reserve in the 1970s.

As an Eagle Scout, Sessions was awarded the Distinguished Eagle Scout

Award. The Scouts' motto, "Be prepared," is on his desk in his Senate office.

He was one of only three senators to vote against additional funding for the Veterans Affairs medical system. He opposed the bill because of cost concerns and indicated that Congress should instead focus on "reforms and solutions that improve the quality of service and the effectiveness that is delivered."

He has taken a strong stance against any immigration reform and believes in the need for a stronger controls on the border with Mexico.

He is anti-abortion, is a major opponent of same-sex marriage and is known for the Victims of Child Abuse Act Reauthorization Act, which would reauthorize funding through 2018 to help victims of child abuse. Sessions said, "There is no higher duty than protecting our nation's children."

Chapter 5

Betsy Devos

Education secretary

The name Devos, I recognized quickly because her father-in-law Rich Devos was the co-founder of Amway. I listened to many of his tapes and heard him make a speech in Charlotte, North Carolina.

DeVos, an education activist in Michigan and a major GOP donor, was confirmed to serve as education secretary after Pence cast a tiebreaking vote in the Senate. It was the first time a vice president broke a tie to confirm a Cabinet nominee.

Betsy DeVos, a Michigan education activist and major GOP donor, has been tapped by President-elect Donald Trump to be his pick for education secretary.

She is an advocate for school choice and charter schools and has drawn criticism in conservative circles for being associated with groups that support the Common Core.

What she does now: Chairwoman of the Windquest Group, a privately held investment and management firm, and American Federation for Children, a school choice advocacy group. Serves on a number of additional boards, including Alliance for School Choice, ArtPrize, Philanthropy Roundtable, Foundation for Excellence in Education, DeVos Institute for Arts Management, Great Lakes Education Project and the Potter's House School.

Family: Married to Dick DeVos — the president of the Windquest Group, an heir to the Amway fortune and a former Republican candidate for governor of Michigan — for over 30 years. She has four children and five grandchildren.

She is one of the most prolific Republican donors in the country. According to the nonpartisan and nonprofit Center for Responsive Politics, DeVos and her husband gave more than $2.75 million to candidates, parties and PACS during the 2016 election cycle.

She contributed to both Jeb Bush and Sen. Marco Rubio's Super PACs during the GOP primary.

DeVos and her husband were the subject of a Mother Jones profile that labeled them the "new Kochs." Billionaire brothers David and Charles Koch have been influential in national politics for decades, donating hundreds of millions of dollars to Republican candidates, think tanks, PACs and more.

While part of a strong Republican family in Michigan, Betsy DeVos has said education should be non-partisan: "What we've tried to do is engage with Democrats, to make it politically safe for them to do what they know in their heart of hearts is the right thing. Education should be non-partisan."

She believes some of her greatest successes have been in Florida's (and to a lesser extent, Louisiana's and Indiana's) education system. "Through its tax-credit scholarship program, Florida has enjoyed the nation's longest period of widespread educational choice, and through the expansion of the program, it has an ever growing number of students — currently over 50,000 — attending the school of their family's choice," she said in 2013.

DeVos met with Trump in Bedminster, New Jersey. The conversation during the meeting with Trump was, according to the transition team, "focused on the Common Core mission and setting higher national standards and promoting the growth of school choice across the nation."

Organizations that DeVos has been a part of supported Common Core, leading some to say that she supported the controversial education standards as well. However, she denies backing the standards. "I am not a supporter — period," she said on her website. "I do support high standards, strong accountability and local control. When governors such as John Engler, Mike Huckabee and Mike Pence were driving the conversation on voluntary high standards driven by local voices, it all made sense," she added.

The Dick and Betsy DeVos Family Foundation is listed on the Clinton Foundation website as a donor — a group Trump lambasted on the campaign trail. The contribution was earmarked "exclusively for CGI activities such as memberships, sponsorships and conference fees."

Chapter 6

Linda McMahon

Small business administrator

The name McMahon brought many stories to my mind. One was particularly interesting. The story dealt mostly with Linda's husband, Vince.

Vince was a promoter as well as a professional wrestler. He wanted Trump to make a speech for him to promote his business activities.

Vince called Trump's office and told the secretary what he wanted. He said, "I am willing to give Trump $10,000.00 to make a one hour speech."

She told him he was wasting her time. She said, "I would not even take the message to him for that small amount."

Vince called back a few days later and told her he would raise the amount to $25,000.00. Her answer was, "You are still wasting my time."

A few days later vince called again and said he was willing to go as much as

$1000,000.00. She said, "I will tell him but I don't think he will be interested."

She gave Trump the message and told him about the other calls. He replied, "This guy sounds interesting, I will give him a call and see what he is up to."

Trump told him right from the start that he didn't make speeches that cheap. Vince really needed Trump to make the speech.

They finally agreed that Vince would pay Trump two million dollars. Vince said later is was worth every penny.

The two became good friends. Some time later Vince wanted to do a promotion with Trump to do a wrestling match. Vince was a professional wrestler. Vince told Trump that they need to appoint a professional wrestler for each of them and the one that lost would get his head shaved by the winner.

At first, Trump argued with Vince. He said, "I am bigger than you. I am stronger than you. I am better looking than you"

They agreed on Vince's plan. Trump's man won the match. While another professional wrestler held Vince, Trump shaved his head. It was a great promotion.

Linda being the CEO of the company was in on all of Trump's and Vince's Arrangements.

Linda McMahon is a co-founder and former CEO of WWE. Before Trump's Dec. 7 announcement that she would be his pick to lead the Small Business Administration, she was an adviser to global businesses as part of APCO Worldwide's International Advisory Council.

She was a top donor to Trump throughout his campaign. She ran for the U.S. Senate seat in Connecticut in 2010 and 2012, losing both times.

Environmental Protection Agency administrator.

President-elect Donald Trump picked Linda McMahon, former CEO of World Wrestling Entertainment, to serve as the administrator of the Small Business Administration, his transition announced Wednesday.

"Linda has a tremendous background and is widely recognized as one of the country's top female executives advising businesses around the globe," Trump said in a statement. "She helped grow WWE from a modest 13-person operation to a publicly traded global enterprise with more than 800 employees in offices worldwide."

He continued, "Linda is going to be a phenomenal leader and champion for small

businesses and unleash America's entrepre-
neurial spirit all across the country."

Chapter 7

Nikki Haley

Ambassador to the U.N.

South Carolina Governor Nikki Haley was confirmed on Jan. 24

Haley, the child of Indian immigrants, brings diversity to the nascent administration but had little international experience as governor of South Carolina. President-elect Donald J. Trump has tapped South Carolina Gov. Nikki Haley to serve as ambassador to the United Nations, a role currently occupied by Samantha Power.

Some Republicans were lukewarm toward him during the campaign season. The media has said that Nikki has little international experience.

Being from South Carolina I can tell you that they are wrong. She traveled internationally bringing industry to this state. She did a very good job especially from Japan.

She is the first female governor of South Carolina, is the youngest governor in the U.S. and was the second person of Indian descent to become a governor in the U.S. (after Bobby Jindal of Louisiana).

She gained national prominence in 2015 when she removed the Confederate battle flag from the South Carolina Capitol grounds.

A somewhat tumultuous history with Trump: But after Trump won, she agreed to meet with him on Nov. 17. The next day, speaking at the Federalist Society, she said his election was a rejection of both parties. "We must accept that Donald Trump's election was not an affirmation of the way Republicans have conducted themselves," she said. "He did not do it by celebrating the Republican Party."

Chapter 8

Wilbur Ross

Secretary of Commerce

I watched the swearing in of Ross on TV. That few minutes was a joy to see and hear.

After he was sworn in by Vice President Mike Pence, he was given the microphone to make a speech. He said about 20 words, then he said, "Let's go to work." I believe that is the kind of attitude we will see in future months.

My first impression of ross was, George Burns without the cigar.

Ross is a billionaire investor and the founder of the investment firm W.L. Ross and Co. He has been described as the king of bankruptcy for his work restructuring failed companies and was a key economic adviser to Trump during his campaign.

The work he does reminds me of Edward in the Pretty Woman movie.

Billionaire investor Wilbur Ross was confirmed as the United States' new secretary of commerce Monday by a 72-27 margin in the Senate.

Ross, 78, made a fortune restructuring failed companies in the manufacturing and steel industries, among others, earning him the name, the "King of Bankruptcy."

Prior to his nomination by President Donald Trump, he worked as chairman and chief strategist of the equity firm W.L. Ross and Co.

Ross is hailed as a hero by some for saving failing industries but critics have likened the business practice to being a "vulture investor," though Ross himself disdains the term, according to a 2004 New York Magazine profile, which also noted that he prefers the description "a phoenix that rebuilds itself from the ashes."

Ross is known for his robust art collection, and once lent a painting by famed Belgian artist René François Ghislain Magritte to the Tate Liverpool and the Albertina in Vienna. Ross owns 25 Magritte paintings reportedly worth $100 million, according to an estimate by Forbes.

Ross' relationship with Trump dates back to the 1990s when he represented investors who were considering whether to remove Trump from his position as head of his Taj Mahal casino in Atlantic City. Ross reportedly was a leading advocate in claiming the casinos would remain profitable if Trump were to stay on. Trump sold his interest in the Trump Taj Mahal in 2009. The casino closed in October of this year after enduring years of losses.

Ross said in March of 2016 that he was planning to vote for Donald Trump.

"I think the reason why the Trump phenomenon has become so important ... is because middle-class and lower-middle-class America has not really benefited by the last 10 to 15 years of economic activity and they're sick and tired of it and they want something different,"

He went on to become a close economic adviser to Trump through his presidential campaign and a public advocate for him in business circles.

As the owner of the Sago mine, Wilbur Ross was accused by miners and their families of ignoring safety regulations that cost the lives of 12 miners in the 2006 Sago mine disaster. Days after the mine explosion, ABC News' Chief Investigative Correspondent Brian Ross had a sit-down interview with the billionaire in which he defended his company's management of the mine even with multiple warning signs in the form of previously -issued safety citations.**

In August of this year, Wilbur Ross' company paid out a $2.3 million civil penalty to the Securities and Exchange Commission after the SEC charged the company for not disclosing its fee practices to funds it advised and to investors. The company paid the fine "without admitting or denying the findings," according to the SEC.

Chapter 9

Tom Price

Secretary of

Health and Human Services

Price is the first health and human services secretary with a medical background since Dr. Louis W. Sullivan, who served under George H.W. Bush from 1989 to 1993. A Republican congressman from Georgia until his appointment, he is a strong critic of the Affordable Care Act and will likely help the Trump administration with its efforts to repeal and replace the health care bill.

Donald Trump has named Rep. Tom Price of Georgia, a strong critic of the Affordable Care Act, as his pick for secretary of health and human services, the president-elect's transition team announced this morning.

Price, the chairman of the House Budget Committee and an orthopedic surgeon, is one of the few Republicans in Congress to have proposed a detailed, conservative alternative to "Obamacare."

In a statement, Trump said Price "is exceptionally qualified to shepherd our commitment to repeal and replace 'Obamacare' and bring affordable and accessible health care to every American."

Price said in a statement, "There is much work to be done to ensure we have a health care system that works for patients, families and doctors."

The Georgia Republican, who met with Trump in New York City earlier this month, was one of the first House committee chairmen to endorse then-candidate Trump, in May as the GOP presidential primaries were ending.

As health and human services secretary, Price would play a major role in any repeal or replacement of "Obamacare" and in any changes to Medicare, which he supports privatizing.

Price was first elected to Congress in 2004 after four terms in the Georgia state Senate. In Congress he served for several years in the House alongside Mike Pence, now the vice-president-elect. Price, like Pence, has served as the chairman of the Republican Study Committee, a large and influential conservative House GOP caucus.

Chapter 10

Elaine Chao

Secretary of transportation

Chao previously served as labor secretary for President George W. Bush and was the only Cabinet official to serve through all eight years of his presidency. She made history as the first Asian-American woman to serve in a U.S. president's Cabinet. Donald Trump has selected Elaine Chao, who was the labor secretary in George W. Bush's administration, to serve as transportation secretary.

Chao, the wife of Senate Majority Leader Mitch McConnell, holds the record of having the longest tenure as labor secretary since World War II, according to her website. She was the only member of Bush's Cabinet to serve all eight years of his presidency. She made history as the first Asian-American woman to serve in a U.S. president's Cabinet.

She is the third woman named by Trump for his Cabinet so far. The others are Betsy DeVos for education secretary and Nikki Haley for ambassador to the United Nations.

She came to the United States at the age of 8. On her website, she writes of herself, "The experience transitioning to a new country has motivated her to dedicate most of her professional life to ensuring that all people have the opportunity to build better lives."

From 2001 to 2009, Chao served as secretary of labor under George W. Bush. Before that, she was the deputy secretary of transportation under George H.W. Bush.

After her time in the first Bush administration, in late 1991 she became the director of the Peace Corps, where she facilitated programs in the Baltic and in newly independent states of the former Soviet Union, according to her website. One year later she was appointed the CEO of United Way of America, replacing William Aramony, who resigned after becoming involved in a financial scandal.

Chapter 11

Steven Mnuchin

Secretary of the treasury

Mnuchin worked for 17 years at Goldman Sachs, where he served as the chief information officer. He founded the investment firm Dune Capital Management and the entertainment financing company RatPac-Dune Entertainment.

Former Goldman Sachs executive and hedge fund CEO Steve Mnuchin was confirmed as the new secretary of the treasury Monday, with a 53-47 vote. Mnuchin previously served as Donald Trump's finance chairman during his presidential campaign.

Over the years, Mnuchin has been a Hollywood producer and a Democratic donor who has faced some controversy: A lending company on whose board he sits, the CIT Group, faces a housing discrimination complaint. "CIT is committed to fair lending and works hard to meet the credit needs of all communities and neighborhoods we serve," the company said in an e-mail to ABC News.

Something you may not know about him: Mnuchin was a member of the exclusive Skull and Bones secret society at Yale, as were George H.W. Bush, George W. Bush and John Kerry.

Trump named Mnuchin as national campaign finance chairman in May 2016. In an interview with Bloomberg, Mnuchin said he was with Trump at Trump Tower the night he won the New York primary and Trump asked him to join his campaign. "He's bringing a lot of people into the party who have not been part of the party in the past," Mnuchin said, according to Bloomberg.

In 2009, Dune Capital was among those that bought interests in a Trump construction project in Chicago. Trump subsequently sued to extend the dates of the loans, which the defendants, including Dune Capital, did not accept.

As treasury secretary, Mnuchin could be influential in the push — promoted by the Trump team — to alter the Dodd-Frank Wall Street regulations.

Mnuchin's mother invested with Bernie Madoff. She died in 2005 and left her sons $5 million. Securities Investor Protection Act Administrator Irving Picard sued them, claiming that $3 million of the money was stolen profits. The lawsuit was ultimately dropped.

Chapter 12

Retired Gen. James Mattis

Secretary of Defense

I was glad to see Mattis win the nomination. His nickname "Mad Dog" indicates the kind of military leader he is.

Mattis retired from the Marine Corps in 2013 after a storied 41-year career that included leading U.S. troops in Afghanistan, Iraq and in Kuwait. He most recently served as the head of U.S. Central Command.

Congress passed a special law to exempt Mattis from the requirement that commissioned officers be out of active duty at least seven years before serving as defense secretary. Within hours of Trump's being sworn in as president, the Senate confirmed Mattis in a 98-1 vote as secretary of defense.

President-elect Donald Trump announced Thursday night that he will "appoint" retired Marine Gen. James "Mad Dog" Mattis to be his secretary of defense.

"We are going to appoint 'Mad Dog' Mattis as our Secretary of Defense," Trump said at a rally in Cincinnati, Ohio. "But we're not announcing it till Monday so don't tell anybody. Mad dog. He's great. He is great."

Under the Appointments Clause of the U.S. Constitution, certain federal positions appointed by the president -- including secretary of defense -- require confirmation of the U.S. Senate.

After their hour-long meeting in November, President-elect Donald Trump described retired Marine Gen. James Mattis — thought to be a contender for defense secretary — as "the real deal."

Mattis retired from the Marine Corps in 2013 after a 41-year career in which he led troops in Kuwait during the Persian Gulf War, in Afghanistan during the initial U.S. wave in 2001 and in Iraq during the 2003 invasion. He capped his career as the head of U.S. Central Command, where he was in charge of all American forces serving in the Middle East and oversaw the wars in Iraq and Afghanistan.

He earned his nicknames Mad Dog and the Warrior Monk for his attention to military tactics and strategy. He is known for his candor and blunt talk, which have at times gotten him into hot water.

Chapter 13

Dr. Ben Carson

Secretary of Housing

and Urban Development

From the beginning when Carson was not getting the votes he needed that he would be name the Surgeon General.

Carson, a retired neurosurgeon, was a Trump rival during the 2016 Republican primaries. He has never held elected office or worked in government.

After his initial hesitation to take a position in a Donald Trump administration, Ben Carson has reconsidered and accepted Trump's offer to be the next secretary of the U.S. Department of Housing and Urban Development.

President-elect Trump announced he intends to nominate Carson for the cabinet position of HUD secretary, a position that will have to be confirmed by the Senate after Trump is in office.

"We have talked at length about my urban renewal agenda and our message of economic revival, very much including our inner cities," Trump said.

"Ben shares my optimism about the future of our country and is part of ensuring that this is a Presidency representing all Americans."

"I feel that I can make a significant contribution particularly by strengthening communities that are most in need," Carson, 65, said in the statement. "We have much work to do in enhancing every aspect of our nation and ensuring that our nation's housing needs are met."

Carson, in an interview with the Washington Post last month, said he'd prefer to "work from the outside and not from the inside."

"I've said that if it came to a point where he absolutely needs me, I'd reconsider. But I don't think that's the situation with these positions,"

A retired celebrated neurosurgeon, Carson was once reported to be a contender for secretary of Health and Human Services, a position Tom Price has filled.

When asked about his qualifications for secretary of HUD, Carson, a Detroit native, "I grew up in the inner city and have spent a lot of time there, and have dealt with a lot of patients from that area and recognize that we cannot have a strong nation if we have weak inner cities."

Chapter 14

Retired General John Kelly
Secretary of Homeland Security

Kelly, age 66 was a four-star general and the head of the U.S. Southern Command. In addition to leading troops overseas, he is known for his strong knowledge of border issues and the drug trade in South and Central America.

President-elect Donald Trump announced that he has selected retired four-star Marine Gen. John Kelly as his pick to lead the Department of Homeland Security.

Kelly, the second general selected for the Cabinet after retired Gen. James Mattis was chosen for defense secretary, first met with the president-elect on Nov. 20 at a Trump-owned golf course in New Jersey.

Kelly was the commander of U.S. Southern Command and a four-star general. As head of Southcom, he was responsible for Guantanamo Bay and all U.S. military operations in South and Central America. At his retirement earlier this year, he was the armed forces' longest-serving general.

Kelly enlisted in the Marine Corps in 1970. His first military deployment was to Guantanamo Bay in 1971 when he was just 20 years old.

In 1999, he served as the special assistant to the supreme allied commander in Europe, one of NATO's two strategic commanders. By 2002, he was promoted to brigadier general and served — mostly in Iraq — with the 1st Marine Division as the assistant division commander.

After three years as a legislative assistant to the Marine Corps commandant in Washington, D.C., Kelly was promoted to major general and returned to Camp Pendleton to command I Marine Expeditionary

Force. During his deployment in 2008 to Iraq's Anbar and western Nineveh provinces, he was a key military player in what became known as the Anbar Awakening, which temporarily reduced sectarian violence.

Kelly is a Gold Star father. His younger son, Marine 1st Lt. Robert Kelly, was killed by an improvised explosive device in Afghanistan in 2010.

While Kelly was prepared to shut down the U.S. detention facility at the direction of President Barack Obama, he did not conceal his strong disagreement with the decision.

Chapter 15

Rep. Ryan Zinke

Secretary of the Interior

Zinke is the former House representative from Montana and a retired Navy SEAL. He's the first interior secretary from Montana.

Donald Trump Jr., an avid hunter and outdoorsman, was involved in selecting the interior secretary, including telephone calls and meetings with candidates, according to a source familiar with the process.

Zinke was the sole Montana representative in the U.S. House in his second term before he was tapped to be interior secretary. He served on the Armed Services Committee and the Committee on Natural Resources.

Zinke was a Navy SEAL from 1986 to 2008. He retired at the rank of commander and was awarded two Bronze Stars for combat missions in Iraq. He was the first Navy SEAL elected to the U.S. House, in 2014, and was in the Montana state Senate from 2009 to 2012, serving on the education and finance and claims committees.

Zinke endorsed Trump for president last May. In November his wife was appointed to Trump's Veterans Administration landing team.

Zinke and Trump met in Trump Tower in New York on Dec. 12, 2016. Zinke said in a message to the Montana newspaper The Billing Gazette, "President-elect Donald Trump and I had a very positive meeting where we discussed a wide range of Montana priorities ... We are both very hopeful for the future."

Chapter 16

Rick Perry

Secretary of Energy

I was impressed with Rick Perry during the primaries.

Donald Trump tapped Perry, a former Texas governor, to lead the federal agency.

President-elect Donald Trump announced his intention to nominate his former rival as his secretary of energy, his transition team announced.

"My administration is going to make sure we take advantage of our huge natural resource deposits to make America energy independent and create vast new wealth for our nation, and Rick Perry is going to do an amazing job as the leader of that process," Trump said in the statement.

Perry announced his second run for president on June 4, 2015, and was the first to drop out of that race, three months later. He was recently a contestant on "Dancing With the Stars," dancing to raise money for veterans, and he was eliminated from the competition in the third week.

With more than 14 years in office, Perry, who succeeded then-President-elect George W. Bush in 2000, was the longest-serving chief executive in Texas history. He had served in statewide office since 1990, as the commissioner of agriculture for two four-year terms and as the lieutenant governor for two years. He spent six years in the Texas House of Representatives.

During the 2012 election season, Trump praised Perry as "a very impressive guy with a very good record."

Chapter 17
David Shulkin
Secretary of Veterans Affairs

Shulkin served as undersecretary of health for the VA under the Obama administration. Shulkin is the first VA secretary in the agency's history not to have served in the military.

David Shulkin, previously an undersecretary at the Department of Veterans Affairs, was unanimously confirmed by the Senate on to lead the agency, which faced criticism during the tenure of President Barack Obama over doctor wait times.

The confirmation was the easiest of Trump's Cabinet appointees thus far, with all 100 senators voting yea.

He was the president at Morristown Medical Center in New Jersey from 2010 to 2015. During that time, he also served in several chief executive roles in the state, at Goryeb Children's Hospital, the Atlantic Rehabilitation Institute and the Atlantic Health System Accountable Care Organization.

He founded a health care information company called DoctorQuality.

Shulkin is married to Merle Bari, a dermatologist, whom he met while doing his residency at the University of

He received his medical degree from the Medical College of Pennsylvania. He did his internship at the Yale University School of Medicine.

Shulkin is not a veteran, but his family has a history of military service and providing military medical care. Both his grandfathers served in World War I. His father was a psychiatrist who was an Army captain, and his grandfather was the chief pharmacist at the VA in Madison, Wisconsin.

In a December interview with USA Today, Shulkin cautioned, "My concern is that veterans are going to see that their hospital is a 'one' in our star system, assume that's bad quality and veterans that need care are not going to get care. And they're going to stay away from hospitals, and that's going to hurt people."

I have been very impressed with all I have read about Shulkin. It appears that we are going to see some big changes in the VA system.

Chapter 18

Former Georgia Governor

Sonny Purdue

Secretary of Agriculture

Perdue, 70, a Republican, served as the governor of Georgia from 2003 to 2011. He worked on Trump's agricultural advisory committee during his presidential campaign.

President-elect Donald Trump tapped former Georgia Gov. Sonny

Perdue for secretary of agriculture.

I am proud and honored to be joining President-elect Trump's administration as his Secretary of Agriculture," Perdue said in a statement released by the Trump transition team.

"Beginning as a simple Georgia farm boy, making sure Americans who make their livelihood in the agriculture industry are thriving is near and dear to my heart, and I'm going to champion the concerns of American agriculture and work tirelessly to solve the issues facing our farm families in this new role."

Perdue's nomination must be confirmed by the Republican-led Senate.

Upon his inauguration in January 2003, he became the first Republican governor of Georgia since Reconstruction.

Chapter 19

Reince Priebus

Chief of staff

This is the only Cabinet-level position that does not need Senate confirmation.

The selection of Priebus as Trump's chief of staff was the first Cabinet-level announcement. Priebus was the chairman of the Republican National Committee until his appointment. President-elect Donald Trump announced he has appointed Reince Priebus as his chief of staff, the first appointment of his incoming administration.

While Trump has run an outsider campaign against the Washington establishment, promising to "drain the swamp" in D.C., Priebus has been in Washington for almost six years leading the Republican National Committee.

His first name rhymes with "pints" and is short for Reinhold. Priebus is pronounced PREE-bus.

Priebus was born in Kenosha, Wisconsin, to Richard and Dimitra Priebus. He is a self-described lifelong

Green Bay Packers fan.

Reince Priebus graduated from the University of Wisconsin at Whitewater in 1994 and received his law degree from the University of Miami School of Law in 1998.

Before he went to Washington he was the national GOP chairman, Priebus worked his way up through the ranks of his home state's Republican Party.

Priebus has been the longest-serving RNC chairman in modern history. He was first elected chairman on Jan. 14, 2011, and inherited an RNC that was $23 million in debt. By the next year, he dug the RNC out of that deep hole, with $20 million in cash on hand, against $13 million in debt.

Trump has praised Priebus' leadership at the RNC, and the two spoke every day when Trump was the GOP nominee. During the primaries, however, there were times when Trump attacked the RNC.

Chapter 20

Rep. Mike Pompeo

CIA Director

Pompeo, who supported Sen. Marco Rubio during the GOP primaries, represented Kansas' 4th Congressional District.

"I am honored to have been given this opportunity to serve and to work alongside President-elect Donald J. Trump to keep America safe," Pompeo said today in a statement. "I also look forward to working with America's intelligence warriors, who do so much to protect Americans each and every day."

Before his 2010 election to represent the district, Pompeo was president of Sentry International, a Midwest company that sells imported pumping units to U.S. gas and oil distributors. Before that, he founded a Wichita, Kansas, company originally known as Thayer Aerospace, which manufactures components for the commercial aerospace, defense and space industries.

After graduating from West Point, Pompeo served as a cavalry officer in the U.S. Army.

As a congressman, Pompeo served on the House Intelligence Committee, conducting oversight of U.S. intelligence agencies, and the House Select Committee on Benghazi. Pompeo and Rep. Jim Jordan, R-Ohio, released in June their own addendum to the House Benghazi Committee report that condemned Hillary Clinton's leadership of the State Department during the deadly Benghazi, Libya, attack, and accused the administration of misleading the public about events there.

The supplement was far more critical than the GOP majority report led by the committee chairman, Rep. Trey Gowdy, R-S.C.

Pompeo opposes the Iran deal, arguing in a summer op-ed that it hasn't helped make the United States safer.

He is opposed to closing the Guantanamo Bay military prison in Cuba, and has also advocating for strengthening U.S. surveillance capabilities.

Chapter 21

Lt. Gen. H.R. McMaster

National security adviser

(Non-Cabinet senior position)

The position of national security adviser became vacant after Michael Flynn resigned. McMaster, a West Point graduate who was awarded the Silver Star during the Gulf War, was chosen by Trump to replace Flynn.

Army Lt. Gen. H.R. McMaster, a West

Point graduate who was awarded the Silver Star during the Gulf War, was chosen to be Donald Trump's new national security adviser, replacing Michael Flynn, who resigned last week following the revelation that he misled Vice President Mike Pence about his conversations with Russia.

McMaster, who will remain on active duty, joins former generals James Mattis, the secretary of Defense, and John Kelly, the secretary of Homeland Security. He's considered a creative thinker in intelligence circles, and his counterinsurgency strategies in Iraq led to the U.S. Army securing the city of Tal Afar in 2005.

He also took a critical look at the prosecution of the Vietnam War for his Ph.D. thesis, which he later published as a book.

Chapter 22

Scott Pruitt
E.P.A. Administrator

The Oklahoma attorney general is a close ally of the fossil fuel industry and has taken on the E.P.A. directly in his current job. He would oversee an agency that the president has vowed to dismantle "in almost every form."

During his hearing, Mr. Pruitt said he disagreed with Mr. Trump's statement that climate change was a "hoax." He criticized federal environmental regulations, emphasizing a states-based approach.

Pruitt begins what is likely to be a controversial tenure with a clear set of goals. He has been outspoken in his view, widely shared by Republicans, that the EPA zealously overstepped its legal authority under President Barack Obama, saddling the fossil-fuel industry with unnecessary and onerous regulations.

But rolling back the environmental actions of the previous administration won't happen quickly or easily. Even if President Trump issues executive orders aimed at undoing Obama initiatives to combat climate change, oversee waterways and wetlands and slash pollution from power plants — as he is expected to do as early as next week — existing regulations won't disappear over-night.

Chapter 23

Dan Coats
Director of National Intelligence

Coats served on the Senate intelligence and armed services committees while representing Indiana. Some in Mr. Trump's orbit believe that the job, overseeing the entire military and civilian intelligence apparatus, is superfluous.

Former senator Dan Coats promised Tuesday to help members of the Senate Intelligence Committee investigate Russia's attempt to influence the presidential election if he's confirmed to be President Trump's director of national intelligence.

"It's a very key issue that we understand fully what has happened and how it's happened," the Indiana Republican said at his confirmation hearing.

Coats, 73, was widely and effusively praised by his former colleagues, as he joked that it was far different being in the witness seat than alongside members of the committee on which he previously served.

But while several senators said Trump couldn't have made a better choice, Sen. Angus King, I-Maine, said his one concern is that Coats might be too nice for the job.

"I'm not sure likeability and affability are the qualities I want in this position," King said. "I want somebody who is crusty and mean and tough because you're riding herd on 17 agencies that will always want to be going in different directions, and you're going to be reporting to a president who may or may not want to hear what you have to say."

"I absolutely understand that this role demands someone who can stand up to the pressures that will be placed upon him," Coats said. "Given the situation that we are facing worldwide in terms of these threats, we don't have time just to be the nice guy."

Coats previously served in the US Senate from 1989 until 1999 before becoming the US ambassador to Germany in the first term of President George W. Bush's administration. He then returned to the Senate after winning election in 2010.

Coats would step into the role at a time

when US intelligence efforts are being intensely scrutinized amid the US intelligence community's conclusions that Russia hacked Democratic Party groups and individuals -- conclusions Trump has repeatedly dismissed.

Chapter 24

Robert E. Lighthizer

Trade Reprehensive

Mr. Trump and his top advisers on trade, including Mr. Lighthizer, share a view that the United States in recent decades prioritized the ideal of free trade over its own self-interest. They argue that other countries are undermining America's industrial base by subsidizing their own export industries while impeding American importers. They regard this unfair competition as a key reason for the lackluster growth of the economy.

Lighthizer, whose selected was first leaked by Trump transition officials, will join a team of Trump lieutenants charged with fulfilling one the central promises of Trump's populist candidacy: aggressively confronting China, Mexico and other nations the president-elect believes have been taking advantage of international trade agreements, to the detriment of U.S. workers.

"We are going to do great things for the American people with Mick Mulvaney leading the Office of Management and Budget," Trump said in a statement. "Right now we are nearly $20 trillion in debt, but Mick is a very high-energy leader with deep convictions for how to responsibly manage our nation's finances and save our country from drowning in red ink.

Chapter 24

Mick Mulvaney

Management & Budget

President-elect Donald Trump has named Rep. Mick Mulvaney (R-S.C.) as his director of the Office of Management and Budget, signaling his intent to slash spending and address the deficit as president.

Mulvaney, 49, was elected to Congress in 2010 in the wave that brought a cohort of younger, staunchly conservative members into the House. Mulvaney quickly staked out ground as one of Congress's most outspoken fiscal hawks — playing a key role in the 2011 showdown between President Obama and House Republicans that ended in the passage of strict budget caps.

He has been an advocate for spending cuts, often taking on his own party to push for more aggressive curbs to government spending.

"We are going to do great things for the American people with Mick Mulvaney leading the Office of Management and Budget," Trump said in a statement. "Right now we are nearly $20 trillion in debt, but Mick is a very high-energy leader with deep convictions for how to responsibly manage our nation's finances and save our country from drowning in red ink.

"With Mick at the head of OMB, my administration is going to make smart choices about America's budget, bring new accountability to our federal government, and renew the American taxpayer's trust in how their money is spent," he added.

Other books by Raymond E. Smith may be viewed at: amazon.com/author/papasbooks